T0167202

ME and THE Monster

Understanding Borderline Personality Disorder

Jason Murra

iUniverse, Inc.
Bloomington

Me and the Monster
Understanding Borderline Personality Disorder

Copyright © 2012 by Jason Murra.

All rights reserved. No part of this book may be used or reproduced by any means, graphic, electronic, or mechanical, including photocopying, recording, taping or by any information storage retrieval system without the written permission of the publisher except in the case of brief quotations embodied in critical articles and reviews.

iUniverse books may be ordered through booksellers or by contacting:

iUniverse
1663 Liberty Drive
Bloomington, IN 47403
www.iuniverse.com
1-800-Authors (1-800-288-4677)

Because of the dynamic nature of the Internet, any web addresses or links contained in this book may have changed since publication and may no longer be valid. The views expressed in this work are solely those of the author and do not necessarily reflect the views of the publisher, and the publisher hereby disclaims any responsibility for them.

Any people depicted in stock imagery provided by Thinkstock are models, and such images are being used for illustrative purposes only.
Certain stock imagery © Thinkstock.

ISBN: 978-1-4620-8321-3 (sc)
ISBN: 978-1-4620-8322-0 (ebk)

Printed in the United States of America

iUniverse rev. date: 12/27/2011

CONTENTS

Chapter 1   What is Borderline Personality Disorder?..... 1

Chapter 2   The Transparent Self.................................... 5

Chapter 3   The Social and Cultural Factors, the
            Development of Borderline Personality
            Disorder 11

Chapter 4   Psychological Factors . . . .
            Is it in Your Head?...................................... 15

Chapter 5   What Causes Borderline Personality
            Disorder?.. 25

Chapter 6   Feelings of Emptiness 31

Chapter 7   The Highly Unstable Mood....................... 35

Chapter 8   The Crushing Feelings of Emptiness.......... 39

Chapter 9   Attempts to Avoid Being in
            Abandonment 43

Chapter 10 The Impulsive Acts..................................... 47

Chapter 11 The Ten Commandments Of Borderline
            Personality Disorder 51

David A. Dill
1965-2000

I dedicate this book to the best friend I ever had.
You taught and gave me so much; I cannot ever
begin to repay you. To a friend, a big brother.
Thank You I will never forget you . . . .
Jason Murra

For all of those who suffer from BPD, I really know what you are going through

Jason Murra 2011

Who would ever cast a negative remark; let them look in the mirror first.

Jason Murra 2010

Mental Illness is a lot like alcoholism, you battle it every day.

Jason Murra 2010

I would like to thank Caroline Sullivan for doing the photo shoots, which are in this book. For with out your talents, none of this would have been possible. God Bless You.

Jason Murra

The Introduction

Hello there I want to thank you for purchasing this book. I think you will find it very informative and friendly to read. Unlike my last book, I have found a disease that affects me, and thousands of others. Help is available by contacting your local counseling center, or health care provider. Just as I have taken the first steps, I urge you to do so.

Jason Murra

CHAPTER 1

What is Borderline Personality Disorder?

Borderline Personality Disorder (BPD) is a way of being in the world that involves mega mood fluctuations; it is associated with intense, stormy relationships, desperation, loneliness, and insecurity. I know you have suffered with these problems, just as I have.

I know for some of us, you feel like you are on top of the world happy go lucky, and then in an instant, you are upset, angry, and moody.

Here is a story that may make sense to you: there is a girl we will call her Jenny, who was on top of the world, or so it seems. She could be happy at times and hot tempered at other times. Jenny knew that her relationship with her boyfriend was going sour. Soon after they broke up, Jenny met some one else at a bar, his name was Dan. They were quite flirtatious when they first met, almost like they knew each other for an extended period of time. By the time the party was over, they had gone to his house where they starred into each others eyes. They made love all night long. They would be together at every free moment they had mostly making love. After only dating a couple of weeks, they went on a vacation, and soon after, they had moved in together.

Now this is where the problem starts; since Jenny moved in, she began to feel trapped inside. She found herself mad and angry toward Dan. She would get angry over the most minor things. As time went on, Dan would distance himself from Jenny, to avoid making a confrontation with her, but this only made Jenny more upset and even more moody. She desperately feared that her relationship was in jeopardy. Even though she was yelling at him, deep inside her she felt scared inside. And at this time they were hardly having sex at all. Then one day Dan came home for lunch. As soon as he walked in the door, Jenny went into a tantrum calling him every name in the book. Her temper lasted for an hour or so, she accused him of cheating on him, as she gave him the finger, and a number of put downs. She threw him out of the apartment.

When Dan Left, Jenny seemed to calm down, but since Dan was gone, she felt anxious and scared to be alone. The apartment seemed cold, dark, dreary, and most of all empty. She was so anxious and scared to be alone. How could she do that? Doesn't he love me any more? Jenny was sinking into the abyss of feeling loneliness and despair. She felt she had made a grave mistake like that. He was a great guy. She started to have a panic attack of fearing she will loose him, so she went looking for him, as the fear and tears ran down her face.

Have you ever been in this situation? This is a clear indication of BPD. This is known as the value and devalue behaviors. I can't tell you how many relationships I have been in where I have wrecked them because of BPD. I remember this one girl I met in 1985. She was a very good girl. I would go and spend the weekends at her parent's house. I would start to dist myself from her. I would have many affairs on her, but when she found out what was going on, she left me for some one else. I felt like she was no good, or trash, and like I needed some one better. When she found out what was going on, she broke up with me. It was at that time I felt alone, empty, I wanted her back. Can you see what I am talking about? It kind of reminds me of that new car smell, but it goes away fast, and you wish you had it back.

CHAPTER 2

The Transparent Self

There is so many what I call "requisites" in our American Culture that encourages the development of BPD. One such behavior is the empty self. According to many psychologists, it's a self that seeks the experience of being filled up by consuming goods, experiences, romantic partners, and empathetic counselors. They are alienated from family and community life, they experience emptiness, loneliness, and the loss of life as they are consumed by BPD. The idea of buying more to feel good is a shallow / temporary high. And of coarse this never really fills the void, so we experience the emptiness, and the ways to fill that void.

In short: Our American culture is like a bag of marbles. Some are good, and some are bad. Most people have values and life styles that bring inner peace, a sense of maturity and a positive health image, and a purpose in life. And there those who unfortunately don't.

Parents that work often come home tired and exhausted, so there is little discipline, or quality time spent with the child. Some parents spoil their children with gifts and luxuries to make up for not spending time with them. And finally there are parents who have a high demanding, or high lime lighted job, so they think of their children as a "problem in the plan", as I call it. This is what I have for the most part, gone through. I never had any discipline, and I could do what I want at any time. I guess this is the reason why I had ATV"S, they were the baby sitter to keep me out of my parents hair. I other words, I was the "throw away child".

TV and other media sources have a very strong impact on personality. The role models and heroes have taken a turn for the worst in our society. Listen to some of this "new age music", they are talking about robbing, raping, and killing some one. It is the same as some of out athletes are going to jail for having an illegal substance, or a gun. I know some were charged with seducing a minor. That's quite shameful in our society, and these people get paid high wages. Look at how it is super glorified as you are nothing if you don't own an expensive SUV, or a sports car. The way how media exemplifies it; it's ok to look lavishly with out a care in the world. You can do what ever you want, no matter how it affects some one else. Individuals who see this type of behavior tend to internalize it, known as modeling. Even at home, modeling exists as well. Ever go to a Head Start Class Room and you see some of the children playing with dolls or a stuff toy? If the toy does something wrong, the child will spank it, or shake it up. How about a boy's father who yells and degrades the mother in front of the child. As he degrades her, hits her, and acts macho. How do you think that boy will turn out? And it could be a girl as well. Our parents and TV play a big role in the modeling of out children. The TV brings out modeling as in making children grow up faster than what we have ever seen. Children are being more sexually active at a younger age, being impulsive, violently angry. Just a short note, look at video games too.

It's unfortunate that marriages are no longer stable as they once were. More than 50% of marriages end in divorce. Some parents tend not to marry, so when the break up happens, its twice as hard to raise the children.

Children of divorce, may often wonder if my family is torn apart, then who is there that I can count on? I'm not saying that divorce is a bad thing, I had to divorce my children's mother, and it was because she was having a serious drug problem. She didn't want to get help, and I knew if I didn't do what I had to do, there would be lasting consequences. I did divorce her in 1995, and she had hardly anything to do with them. They were at the ages of 2 & 4. It is now 2010, my oldest was graduating; he had told me their mom was coming up to see my son graduate. She promised she would be there. In April of 2010, their mother had died of a drug over dose. Can you imagine what my kids have gone through?

And I'm not saying to stay in a dysfunctional relationship either. I found out that myself, its better to leave a bad situation, than to stay in one. No matter if its violence, alcoholism, drug abuse, or some other addictive behavior. This can all lead to BPD. I personally don't believe my BPD was caused by one single incident, but rather genetic, and traumatic experiences.

Children suffer in many ways, since the child feels as if there is no one to turn to, who can I count on? How can I trust my impressions of other people? If there is trust broken, and abuse, children will develop BPD. I know children can have a hard time being raised by one parent. I know it's hard, but I did it. I STRONGLY URGE YOU TO TELL YOUR CHILDREN AT LEAST 15X A DAY POSITIVE STATEMENTS LIKE: I LOVE YOU, I AM SO HAPPY I HAVE YOU, YOU ARE THE GREATEST KID/ KIDS A DAD/ MOM COULD EVER HAVE. ALWAYS SAY POSITIVE THINGS TO THEM NO MATTER HOW MUCH THEY MESS UP. I ALSO SUGGEST READING TO YOUR CHILDREN EVERY NIGHT. IT DOSEN'T HAVE TO BE A LONG BOOK. MAKE IT AS FUN FOR YOU AS IT IS FUN FOR THEM. HAVE MOVIE NIGHT AT HOME. I EVEN URGE YOU TO SLEEP WITH YOUR CHILDREN. MY CHILDREN HAVE SLEPT WITH ME UNTIL THE SIXTH GRADE.

Today children are often raised with a multiple array of others; such as day care, grand parents, uncles, aunts, and neighbors.

Those who have experienced sexual abuse, often always feel shame, dirty, and useless. The low self esteem can affect their relationships with friends, but intimate relationships as well. Individuals with BPD have a constant need for dependency, with the fear of abandonment, which runs out of control, which leads to suicidal tendencies, and depression.

When you encounter a person with BPD, one might think they were subjected to abuse, neglect, and have hard feelings toward the family. This can be a huge mistake towards the family. Some off spring that has BPD, come from good families. Children can have biological differences, which cause the disorder. Many types can account for the development of BPD; it can affect every one, the individuals who have it, and those who are around them.

The last way I believe you can get BPD is by bullying. I firmly stand on the subject, that kids, who are harassed in school, will develop BPD. Think about it; if a child lives in fear, and abuse at school, it only makes sense bullying will cause BPD. SO I URGE YOU ALL TO TALK ABOUT BULLYING.

Because if we don't start educating our children and parents, when?

CHAPTER 3

The Social and Cultural Factors, the Development of Borderline Personality Disorder

Evidence does show that BPD is increasing. This may be due to increased awareness and diagnosis of BPD by physicians.

One problem that you can point a finger of blame is an ever accelerating pace of change in our country. Even as a Sociologist, I have developed a model that in every 25 years, look at how much our world has changed. It wasn't about 10 years ago the cell phone has taken over our world. Remember when they first came out, they were called car phones, now look at what they can do. And how about the computer? I confess they are very nice comforts, but what did we do before we had them? Look at the way how jobs are in our world. All you needed was a high school diploma, and I know some of our relatives didn't even have a high school education, but yes yet able to sustain a job until they retired. Jobs were more "hands on learning". I can relate from a personal experience a lot of things are over whelming for people with BPD. Our world is an ever accelerating pace of change. The majority of Americans are affected by this pace of change. In our mobile society, it is becoming less and less that children will grow up in one stable environment. And they are the ones who suffer and can become predisposition to BPD. The constant chaos of every day life can have consequences on all ages of people.

I can remember back in the 80's, I was watching the news show 20/20, and they were doing this story about a home less man. I don't remember where he was from, but he lived under a tunnel. He would go out and pick up pop cans to buy himself some food. The news anchor asked him "why do you live like this"? The man said "because I can't deal with society, I just don't fit in". Now as a Professional that is a clear characteristic of BPD. People with this disease tend to isolate themselves; they stay in their own little bubble of safety. Some people have been tormented in life, that the reason why they are, can you blame them? When you tell your children not to cry; to suck it up, and not to show their emotions, or make them not to show love and affection. Being happy because you did well in school, not giving praise, or saying big deal. When you do things like that to your children, they don't know how to express themselves emotionally, and as a result, they pull themselves away from society. Not being able to express your emotions leads to abandonment. Believe me I was feeling this since I was five years old, and I still feel this way at 42. This is another characteristic of BPD, feeling a transient life, remember the guy on 20/20? Can you see a correlation?

Another form of invalidation to occurs when a child tells some one about the abuse and its not believed, or over looked. Evidence proves that this may be the most powerful impact of all. And since the abuse is seldom is seldom acknowledge by the other family members, and if they were to report it, they run the risks of being blamed, or disbelieved. Do you know how crushing that is to a child, or adolescent? I'm sure we all remember the priest sex scandals? Do you know what it is like for those children to have to live with that? It doesn't go away, and I am sure this has been going on for many years. When children get traumatized like that at an early age, they seldom ever recover, but they have to live with the best with what's been done.

The sexual abuse connects too many of the symptoms of BPD. I have been sexually abused, many times, for many years, and I know what it feels like to be kicked to the curb. For example, children who have experienced incest will often use dissociation to help with the pain from a frightening environment.

CHAPTER 4

Psychological Factors . . . .
Is it in Your Head?

Many psychological factors can enhance the development of BPD. The most researched or discussed are a history of traumatic abuse, the environment, and cultural factors.

One of the most compelling facts is that adults with BPD; have had sexual abuse, physical abuse, and other forms of abuse. If you have read my first book you will know what I am talking about. I urge you to read that book, even if you don't have BPD, you will have a better understanding of what some one has to go through to get BPD. Remember that not all people who have been sexually molested get BPD. It does show how that 2/3 to ¾ of people who have been sexually molested acquire BPD. And know this is not all the people with the disorder have been sexually abused. Invalidations mean that some one is telling you that your feelings, thoughts, or input does not matter or count, what a negative constraint. When you are made to feel inferior, you tend to slip away people and society. This is a valid feeling I have felt most of my life. I call this "The transparent Person". It's like you can walk around, and nobody notices you, or acknowledges you. It's like you don't know who or what you are. Your life is filled with confusion. That was the reason why I didn't go to a special friend's funeral; I felt like nobody liked me, and that I was not wanted, but when you are told that constantly, what do you think the outcome will be? Memory problems; encoding can lead to problems in school, which can lead to teasing, or bullying from class mates, and possibly from teachers. Can you imagine being criticized at home, then getting the same treatment from teachers and peers at Catholic School? This teacher Mary Brien would make me get in front of the class; go to the bathroom and wash my hands, and then say derogatory comments: "you really take the cake Jason", "AINT IS NOT A WORD". Maybe that's why I started to skip school in the 4th grade. I often wonder if this is the reason why I keep asking and girl that I'm involved with, "are you mad at me"? I have a very strong feeling those with BPD, tend to go out at night; I'm not saying the night life, but rather there are less people out in public, and they are more like night owls.

I would like to back to the brain, as you may recall that brain functioning and learning styles can contribute to BPD. Visual intake and discrimination can lead to difficulties interpretation of information from the environment. The person with BPD sees something that they may not be able to select what is important, which makes the situation confusing. Having poor boundaries, is a most definite characteristic of BPD.

People with BPD seem to have difficulty with verbal; visual memory, especially when it comes to complex tasks, which makes it difficult for them to learn from their experiences. They also make the same mistake over and over; such as in relationships, and employment. Information can't be encoded properly will lead to misrepresentations indefinitely.

Brain scan studies show that individuals have difficulty with impulse control, aggression, and have reduced levels of activity in the brain in several locations. Increase in aggression is associated with low levels of activity in the frontal of the cortex, as well as reduced activity within the limbic system. Aggression has been associated with low levels of serotonin as well.

The notion that's says biology plays a minor role in personality, are quite mistaken. Scientific evidence suggests other wise that biological factors are a very important aspect in determining some one who has BPD.

This past decade has given us many exciting findings in our understanding of the neurobiology of personality disorders, and I am very confident that biologists will uncover more.

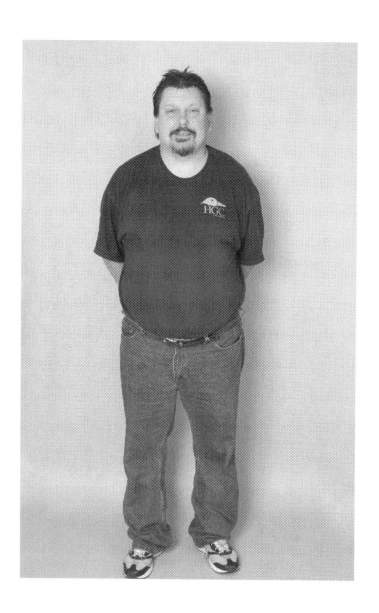

CHAPTER 5

What Causes Borderline Personality Disorder?

BPD is manifested by; biological, psychological, and social factors. This is once again where "bullying" can come into play.

Let's understand that almost all parent house holds have more than one child, and there can be noticeable differences, which can be present from the moment at birth. Remember this can be genetic. One child can be calm, and the other child can be whiney.

In the modern age, we consider BPD to be a distinct pattern of its own. The most common characteristic of BPD is the emotional roller coaster that individuals experience. Cycloid refers to the rapidly cycling emotions and "erratic" that describes the unpredictability of behavior. Liable impulsive disorder is an accurate and concrete description. The name: "borderline" does evoke an image of some one being on the edge. It's the chaotic emotions endured by individuals with the disorder. Inborn characteristics are known as temperaments. Temperament can be defined as "the individual's constitutional disposition to an activity and emotionality". The powerful impact of biology on our own interests; talents, predictions, and personality.

The past 10-15 years has brought many exciting developments in our understanding of the neurobiology of personality disorders. Despite what our parent's were observing, not long ago, there were no biological study of personality. That's because personality thought to be a function of the environment, unlike depression, schizophrenia, and other disorders, which were believed to have biological motives.

The environment is the primary determination of one's life course. Sigmund Freud had come to believe that people's problems were primarily rooted in early child hood experiences, especially how they were raised by their parents, and how they resolved their early conflicts.

The belief that biology plays only a minor role in personality is quite mistaken. Scientific evidence is mounting that biological factors are crucial. The only data strongly suggests that parents react to their children according to their temperaments, as do many others in the individual's environment. Of the portion that cannot be attributed to the biological factors, many factors such as the child's peer interactions; relationships with teachers, and other people of the community, play a huge role in shaping the ultimate personality of the individual. They may act, think, or possible feel like a young child, while those around expect them to act like an adult. They may have the need to act like a child in order to keep them safe. Under stress, in certain circumstances that remind an individual of a traumatic event, the person becomes prone to dissociation.

Even though one might think that dissociation may sound weird, it's really a normal and common function by most people to a lesser degree by every one. Have you ever experienced this: You're at work and while you're at your computer, you look outside its nice outside, and you start to think about the upcoming weekend, and TADA! There you go you have experienced dissociation, but to a lesser degree of course. Another name for it is called "spacing out". This happened for people with BPD to the extent they feel others are out to get them, hurt them. Because of this dissociation, they exhibit loss of awareness, time or self identity. These episodes are very distressing to the person. Dissociation can be thought of as "I'm loosing my mind", or I'm having a nervous breakdown?

I wrote a poem, which is in my first book. It is how I feel I live with BPD.

I sit the night and stare, but the mirror tells me lies. It makes me be things I do not want. It lives inside my mind. Will this thing kill my heart? What does it want from me? Does it want to be let out? Or is it burrowing inside of me?

As I stated in the poem, dissociation disorders are often associated with abuse. Dissociation is an adaptive response by people experiencing something over whelming and that they are powerless to change. A person who is being sexually abused may "disappear" mentally when the abuse is taking place, and quite possibly not being able to remember it at a later time. If the abuse is mild and frequent, less harm may result. Also, individuals who have had other validating and supportive relationships are less likely to have long term effects. For the individuals who were more severely abused, who have strong biological dispositions, or who had little to no support, dissociation is a way of a coping skill that becomes ingrained, and can have chronic problems in functioning.

When I was a therapist, I can understand their feelings of emptiness. I have dealt with many people, to which I can identify from a personal stand point. Over time it started to take control of my life; slow at first, but it grew to an enormous monster, that I couldn't hold my job. I ended up having to go to the psych hospital many times, but it wasn't until 2003 that I finally got a diagnosis of BPD, at the same time my marriage was ruined. Keep reading in the next section: Living With the Monster, I will explain more, but I will say this is my empathetic reactions was nearly identical to the client with BPD. I might find myself pinching myself, and may other mutilation to claim the

Jason Murra

feeling; even pain is better nothing or emptiness. People with BPD will often describe feelings of fear and terror, to the threat of nonexistence (different from, but closely related to a fear of death), and the feelings of vulnerability. I have experienced this.

CHAPTER 6

Feelings of Emptiness

Have you ever experienced feelings of emptiness? If you have never experienced feelings of emptiness, then it's kind of hard to describe it. Some may say it is like seeing the color blue all of the time. For people with BPD, it can happen at any time, it can be a mood altering feeling. Things can trigger it; such as the time of day, a certain day. For me it feels like 1000 knives that are extremely cold pierce my spirit, and my soul.

The best way to describe the emptiness felt by those with BPD is through analogies and metaphors. Many people with BPD do things in either a complete or partial state of dissociations. To me this is the worst feeling a person with BPD can experience.

CHAPTER 7

The Highly Unstable Mood

For people with BPD, it is not uncommon for feelings to swing (Like on a roller coaster) going from thrilled, excited, to king of the world, then down to suicidal, depressed in a matter of a few hours, but it can in some instances go in and out of behaviors in just minutes, this is called "Rapid Cycling". They may experience overwhelming anxiety, and then feel fine. Those mood swings are considered to be the crem della crem of BPD. People with BPD have a hard functioning in the real world, and dissociation thought means of self injury to escape the pain is very much a reality. And this is the reason why people with BPD get picked on a lot by members of society.

Individuals who are told or led to believe by people close to them; they are bad, no good, terrible, or inadequate will internalize these criticisms. Highly severe peer rejection can be just as devastating and is more likely to be over looked as a source of the problem. In other words, it's not taken as real. The clearest abuse is BULLYING. This is giving credence to a high rate of suicidal Idealization. It is very likely that who are prone to BPD, is engulfed by peer rejection and BULLYING. I am glad we have people like Ellen DeGeneres, who are taking an active role in making this aware.

As I have said, suicide is very real for people with BPD, and some people with BPD go to the extreme, and what I mean by that, they may want to make a revenge to make others feel sorry for what they did to them, or not do to them. To escape an intolerable life situation, or to save others from the pain, suffering, and money, that suicide may be the answer, (I DO NOT RECOMMEND SUICIDE AT ALL). I know we all remember the school shootings on the news. Do you think those children just woke up and decided "let's have a school shooting"? It was mental abuse, which was probably done at school "BULLYING". Psycho therapy is one of the best defenses in suicide prevention for people with BPD.

For a lot of people with BPD, most of the symptoms are quite similar. One person describes BPD: I feel like I'm a pressure cooker that's going to explode. Cutting biting myself is like letting the steam out. If I do this, I feel immediate relief.

Chapter 8

The Crushing Feelings of Emptiness

If you have ever experienced feelings of emptiness, then it's very hard to describe the inner hollowness. The desire to be dead among borderline individuals is a very real and often thought of because their lives are so unbearable. The problem is that the person has so many life stressors, problems with personal relationships, employment problems and or physical abuse, which can impair a way to find and enjoy, and give meaning to life its self.

Individuals who were told, or are told, or led to believe by people close to them that they are bad, no good, terrible, internalize these criticisms. Severe peer rejections can be just as devastating and is more likely to be over looked as the source of the problem. Luckily "BULLYING" is now being looked at in schools, and we have also taken an approach to educating people as well. Remember educating is the BEST way to stop BULLYING.

A study has shown that suicidal behavior is often inadvertently rewarded by others. A test called by the "DBT", Dialectical Behavior Therapy, like wise targets patients expectations about the value of suicidal behavior as a problem solving alternative. It's unfortunate that many of these may be quite accurate. If a patients wants to get revenge, or to make others sorry for what the have done, or did not do, even to escape an intolerable life situation, or even save others pain, suffering, and money, suicide may be the answer in their minds. I DO NOT SUGGEST SUICIDE, IT'S NOT WORTH IT. IF YOU KNOW OF SOME ONE IN THIS SITUATION, CALL 911 IMMEDIATELY. Walking away from some one in this state is not acceptable in any way. Get the individual into counseling, even if the require hospitalization. Taking a stand is the key. Showing you care is the best thing you can do. Remember psychotherapy can help the individual a lot. A comprehensive plan along with coping strategies can make a world of difference.

Self injury is one of the more perplexing symptoms of BPD. I know a lot of people would say, "How can they do that to themselves"? (SIB) self injurious behavior is a behavior that a person does to themselves to release pressure no matter how bad it hurts. The individual may feel relief; to make themselves feel better, to escape self hatred, and to cope with memories of abuse, and to block out feelings.

I have empathetic reasons that are identical since I have BPD, I have many urges to do the same things as I have described. I am sorry if I am making this redundant, but I want to give you a general perspective of what it is like for some one living with BPD. It really is bad when you live in fear; terror, being non existent, fear of abandonment, and fear of being abandoned, homeless, or transient.

CHAPTER 9

Attempts to Avoid Being in Abandonment

No one likes to feel abandoned, or have a relationship end. For most people when that happens, there is a time of grievance, and an adjustment period. In time they adjust to the new situation, and go on with their lives. For a person with BPD, the reaction can be much worse. Often there's a cycle of impulsivity. Breaking up with some one, they have regret; remorse, and making desperate attempts to win that person back. Many times the person will fantasize about being with some one else, then make attempts to break up with that person, (not really wanting to break up, but when it does happen, they will try anything to win them back). These processes are known as the value / devalue. The person with BPD may threaten to kill themselves in order to show love. I also think it is to show fear to the individual that they mean business. Sometimes it works, and sometimes it doesn't. And I must say this; it can work both ways too, a person who is the significant other who has BPD, may think they are doing 'what's' right by trying not to trigger events that can lead to a catastrophe. This person is called the enabler. The enabler exists in many dysfunctional relationships. And in my opinion, you're not helping any one, even yourself.

CHAPTER 10

The Impulsive Acts

With people that have BPD, this is a very serious issue, not only financially, but mentally and biological effects as well.

Individuals with BPD live in a hell with their impulses. Many people may resort to alcohol, which can end up with criminal offences. And it can be a financial or medical loss. Some yet may do drugs, which can lead to harder substances, expensive habit, and can land you in jail. Having sex with multiple partners, which can lead to many failed relationships, unwanted pregnancies, and contracting a multitude of diseases . . . . Even HIV. There's another problem BPD people can experience and that is the impulsion to buy things. Many of these people buy things to make them feel good. It is a temporary high, and usually it is something they don't need. Again as I have mentioned earlier; it's just a way to escape pain of what they are going through. Like people watch a movie to escape the problems and to fantasize, and dream. People with BPD almost always have to be doing something to escape their problems. It is very sad to have to live like that. And I feel for all of you. I know I don't have to get into depth about the impulsive acts, just use your imagination.

CHAPTER 11

The Ten Commandments
Of Borderline Personality
Disorder

THE SYMPTOMS OF
BOARDERLINE PERSONALITY DISORDER:

According to the Diagnostic and Statistical Manual of Mental Disorders Fourth Edition (DSMHV) a diagnosis of Borderline Personality Disorder required the presence in the individual must have five or more of the criteria.

1. Makes desperate attempts to avoid abandonment.

2. Had unstable and intense relationships, usually involving alternately idealizing then devaluing the other person.

3. Sense of self of self—The image is chronically unstable.

4. Acts on impulses in ways that can be self damaging for example; overspending, over eating, acting out sexually, and abusing drugs and alcohol.

5. Makes frequent suicidal gestures; threats, or injuries to carry out an act to himself/herself.

6. Has a highly unstable mood, for example, gets depressed, irritable, or anxious for brief periods.

7. Chronically experiences feelings of emptiness.

8. Is easily angered or raged.

9. Under stress can become paranoid, or experience dissociate symptoms.

10. This presentation suggests that a person having five or more of these features may qualify for a diagnosis of BPD.

The end.

The Diagrams:

With the so called "normal people", may have days where they do get stresses, angry, or depressed, but they live mostly in a "gray" area.

The typical day of a person with out BPD.

The typical day of a person with BPD.

It is best to live your life in the "gray areas".

LIVING WITH THE MONSTER‒

This section is my personal account of living with BPD. I have done a lot of research on this disease. It mainly happens to people in their 20's, 30', and 40's, but mine happened, or I should say I noticed it at the age of four. I could just tell by certain emotions I had in certain places even at that age. Maybe that's why I couldn't stay at people's houses, because I felt abandoned. I mean it is weird to be able to decipher this at such a young age. I can remember on a Saturday at my sisters in Iron Mountain, it was Saturday evening, as the sun was starting to set, I was at the play ground on a slide, when these two kids that I knew walked by. It was like an instant my mood whet to this chilled abandoned feeling.

Growing up, was very hard for me not only growing up in an abusive—chaotic house. I felt different from people my age. I did a lot of hiding from people, and of course the way I was treated in the Catholic School that just even added to the fire. I hated school; I almost never finished school, if it wasn't for my welding teacher Bob Justice. I told him I was quitting school, and he said, "Why" he was the only teacher who actually cared about me. When I went to his class, I had somewhat of a self esteem. It was nice to have some one who believed in me.

Going through school was a literal hell. In the 3rd grade I went to West Wood and in that year I think I missed 60 days. I had such a high anxiety about that school, I can remember vomiting in the bathroom because of it. I was told this school was a bad school, and I would get beaten up going there. Can you see how this disease got reinforced?

In high school that was just a joke with all of the negativity I had to go through. I've ruined so many relationships in school. I had a very nice girl in school, we were very serious and then another girl wanted to date me. I went through the value/devalue. I started to see this girl behind my girlfriends back. I kept it up as to when she found out, she broke up with me. I then wanted her back very badly. The crushing feelings of emptiness and the fear of abandonment were red lining. This has happened to many relationships. I have done things that I now regret, but you must understand it's not my fault, but I took steps to understand and to make my life better. Like I have said: with any mental illness, it's a lot like alcoholism, you battle it every day. And a couple more notes on relationships; my first wife was done because of BPD, and then I was dating a girl after I got divorced for about three years, then I met this other girl and then I did the value/ devalue, and like boom, I woke up in Rapid River. It was like "how did I get here"? I had all of those distortions, and I had many anxiety attacks. She was a very nice lady, but I should have not gotten involved with her. Living up there was a total hell, but what was I to do. One thing that has bothered me was that we were living in the country, and my boys were from the city. There weren't many kids for them to play with, and that hurt me very much. But I guess maybe if my sister wouldn't have called me and said "Yea! Do those kids have any friends up there"? There was such a change. I know it's hard for people with BPD to have change, especially when it's an environmental one.

Virtually everything a person with BPD can have, I've had then all. Even in my working life, was very impossible with my condition. In many jobs, I would constantly as "how am I doing"? It had got really bad to where I can not work any more. The last straw as a counselor, the things my clients would tell me was like looking in the mirror, I had many anxiety attacks, which I had to be retired. Life has not been very fun at this time for me.

GOOD BYE TO THE MONSTER

Well here I am almost 43 and what have I done to combat this problem? Well first off I have been in counseling. I go there at least once a week, it took a long time for me to find a good counselor, and if you are going to start counseling, it is best to find one that you can truly open up to, because if you don't feel comfortable opening up your feelings, then how do you expect to feel better? I also attend a BPD group, that is a great way for you to meet other people who have this disease, and you can learn a lot from not only the other people, but you will have certain exercises to work on with yourself.

I myself will be giving public lectures on this disease, to many schools through out the Upper Peninsula of Michigan. I might even start my own website.

In short: I am a person affected by BPD, it has taken my life for many years, but now I am taking BPD. I will be in counseling for the rest of my life, and probably be attending groups as well. I will also be on medicine for the rest of my life. I do believe if you work really hard at going to counseling, going to group, taking your meds, and practicing what you have been told. I think you will have a MUCH better quality of life for you, and the people around you. Isn't that what you want, the monster gone?

The end.